MOZART
AND THE SONATA FORM

Da Capo Press Music Reprint Series

GENERAL EDITOR

FREDERICK FREEDMAN

VASSAR COLLEGE

MOZART
AND THE SONATA FORM

BY J. RAYMOND TOBIN

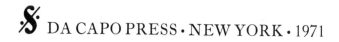 DA CAPO PRESS · NEW YORK · 1971

A Da Capo Press Reprint Edition

This Da Capo Press edition of
Mozart and the Sonata Form
is an unabridged republication of the first
edition published in London in 1916.

Library of Congress Catalog Card Number 76-125063
SBN 306-70027-1

Published by Da Capo Press
A Division of Plenum Publishing Corporation
227 West 17th Street, New York, N.Y. 10011
All Rights Reserved

Manufactured in the United States of America

For Distribution and Sale Only in the
United States of America

MOZART
AND THE SONATA FORM

MOZART
AND THE SONATA FORM

A COMPANION BOOK TO ANY EDITION OF
MOZART'S PIANO SONATAS—INCLUDING AN
ANALYSIS OF THE FORM OF EACH MOVEMENT,
WITH NOTES UPON TREATMENT & TONALITY

BY

J. RAYMOND TOBIN, MUS.B:

(Author of Primer on " Figured-Bass Playing," etc.)

LONDON
WILLIAM REEVES, 83 CHARING CROSS ROAD, W.C.

PRINTED BY THE NEW TEMPLE PRESS, NORBURY CRESCENT, S.W.

CONTENTS

FOREWORD.

FOREWORD

WITH the increasing attention which of recent years has been directed towards the study of design in music, particularly by that large body of executants who realise the value of such knowledge as a guide to true appreciation and correct interpretation, it would seem that a need has arisen for a definite analysis of sonatas other than those of Beethoven. Granted that Bach and Beethoven are the Old and New Testament of music respectively, other reading material is necessary.

Printed analyses of the works of the great masters may have proved inimical to the true interests of the art and encouraged a superficial knowledge and cramming of facts more expedient than helpful, but that is only so when the twenty-four inch guage has been applied without the employment of the mental ear. A consideration of the fundamental principles of design or plan and an examination of their application by each of the great masters—*not least Mozart*—must be extremely beneficial.

The sonatas of Mozart belong to an earlier period than those of Beethoven, and whatever opinion may be expressed upon their thematic or harmonic basis, *the fact must not be overlooked that Mozart's genius and mastery of form as displayed in his compositions afford many problems the elucidation of which cannot fail to be of distinct value to the student mind*, for the power of Mozart in this direction can only be compared with the remarkable diversity of rhythm displayed by Haydn or the infinite resource which characterises the "development" sections of Beethoven.

The important part which Mozart played in the perfecting of almost every musical structure is not sufficiently realised; or if realised, not acknowledged. Haydn and Beethoven on either side, the one proclaimed as founder, the other as perfecter of the sonata form have, in this direction, hidden him somewhat from view: but those who have studied Mozart know how deeply Beethoven even with his phenomenal genius lies indebted to his predecessor and how vital are the lessons to be drawn from the works of Mozart. Though not possessed of the bold initiative of the later master, Mozart was no mere follower of other models; he could and he did think for himself, as is evidenced by his excellent work in regard to the rondo form. One authority declares that Beethoven found the rondo with *one* subject and left it with *two*: the student of *Mozart* knows better. In this connection Stewart Macpherson says: "It is a noteworthy fact that there is hardly a single feature in the form of Beethoven's movements that had not been previously suggested in the works of .... *Mozart.* Two things usually regarded as inventions of Beethoven, viz., the coda and the form known as the rondo sonata are not really attributable to him in the first place at all, being clearly foreshadowed in the works of his predecessors."* Few writers are so wise or so just!

It is sometimes remarked anent the sonatas of Mozart that they lack that continuity which marks the work of his successors—that in fact the various sections are disjointed. Without waiting to inquire if an artist, such as Mozart admittedly was, could have tolerated a creation where the parts did not succeed each other according to artistic rule, it may be noted that the merging of subject into bridge passage, the delightfully insinuating return of the subject matter and many other points so greatly appreciated by the present day student would not have been possible of introduction, even by such a master as Beethoven had not his predecessors by their "disjointed" efforts made the outlines of the form easily recognisable— and therefore in time so familiar.

It might be of interest here to note that in the recapitulatory section of the sonata form, Mozart in one instance makes the entry of the second subject precede that of the first subject; recapitulates the first subject

---

* "Form in Music." Stewart Macpherson, F.R.A.M.

in a key other than the tonic; alters the matter of the second subject and dispenses with the bridge passage: all structural peculiarities which genius dictated and his followers imitated.

Realising the total inadequacy of the old rondo form as a conclusion to the cyclic form, Mozart constantly strove for the light; hence, his employment of the sonata form as a finale in many of the sonatas; his introduction of the fugal form into the "Magic Flute" overture and "Jupiter" symphony; and finally, his presentation of the rondo sonata form, to all intents and purposes as we have it to-day. An examination of the truly magnificent concluding movements of sonatas Nos. 3, 8, 9 and 13 among others will prove the truth of this last assertion. For these reasons then, I have ventured to write these words on musical analysis, feeling that they will form an acceptable supplement to the many admirable treatises on the subject already existing.

And here, I would plead for the training of the "seeing ear" and "hearing eye" in regard to the formal shape, as well as the melodic outline and harmonic structure of a composition. Analysis, such as is here dealt with, will, to some, seem to emanate from the dissecting room of the pedantic musician: such people stand in need of special enlightment, for out of their own mouths they are condemned. True: an arbitrary type of destruction or dismemberment has too often been accepted as analysis, but there is little danger of this if the subject be approached with a desire to obtain a clearer insight and wider understanding of the master and his creation. Rather will it lead to intelligent application in interpretation; a due balancing and subordination of phrases and an appreciation of their extent and relative importance; clarity in the expositions of the various sections; and a purposeful working toward the climax points. Then the pursuit of musical analysis will not be the dissecting of a dead body, but a process which must lead us to the heart of a living thing. It is surely as pleasurable, profitable and illuminating to analyse a musical creation worthy of the time expended, as to examine the calyx, petals, stamens, pistils, pollen and seed of flowers.

TABLE SHOWING THE NUMBERING OF THE SONATAS IN VARIOUS EDITIONS.

ZIMMERMANN & PAUER.	COTTA.	PETERS.	CHAPPELL. HALLE'S.	LITOLFF.	BOSWORTH
Sonata:					
C major, No. 1	5	16	4	11	2
F major, No. 2	6	11	14	5	15
B flat, No. 3	8	17	5	12	18
E flat, No. 4		9	13	10	19
G major, No. 5	2	14	11	4	8
D major, No. 6	15	10	9	13	10
C major, No. 7	11	8	6	6	4
A minor, No. 8	16	7	10	16	7
D major, No. 9	13	3	7	9	9
C major, No. 10	3	2	1	7	3
A major, No. 11	9	12	2	14	12
F major, No. 12	7	6	3	3	13
B flat, No. 13	10	4	8	8	17
C minor, No. 14	18	18	16	18	5 and 6
F major, No. 15	17	1	18	17	16
C major, No. 16	1	15	19	2	1
F major, No. 17	4	5	15	1	14
B flat, No. 18			20		
D major, No. 19	14	13	21	15	11
B flat, No. 20	12		12		

THE CHARACTER AND PLAN OF THE
MOZART SONATA.

THE CHARACTER AND PLAN OF THE
MOZART SONATA.

I.—The references are to the **ZIMMERMANN** (Novello) edition of the sonatas. In numbering the bars each portion of a bar at the commencement of a movement has been regarded as bar one, and wherever, subsequently, a complete bar has been divided by a double bar, the divisions have been indicated so: e.g., 57a; 57b. The small figures denote the beat of the bar. Repeats have been ignored. See list, page 8.

THE sonata of Mozart may be said to consist of three movements, the only exceptions being No. 20, in B flat, which is in four movements, and No. 17, in F major, containing but two movements. The character and sequence of the movements as follows:

(1). An "Allegro" in sonata form: with the exception of No. 4, in E flat*, and No. 11, in A major, which open with an "Adagio" and "Air with Variations" respectively, all these sonatas begin so.

(2). An "Adagio" or "Andante"—a slow move-

---

* As a tonal centre, Mozart never exceeds three sharps or three flats in these sonatas.

11

ment rather than a minuet and trio. Mozart only employs this latter form in three of his pianoforte sonatas, as evidence perchance that in regard to this particular form he *felt* what the greater power of Beethoven effected by the introduction of the scherzo. Mozart's repeated use of the subdominant key for this middle movement should be noted. No less than eleven of the sonatas follow this key scheme. The exceptions are No. 2, in F, where the tonic minor key is employed; Nos. 4, 6, 16 and 19 (dominant key); No. 8 (submediant major): Nos. 11 and 17 (tonic and subdominant keys); and No. 14 (relative major).

(3). An "Allegro" or "Presto" in sonata or rondo form, the only exception being No. 6, in D major, which concludes with an "Air with Variations."

THE FIRST MOVEMENT.

The plan of this form—statement, amplification and re-statement or exposition, development and recapitulation—is so familiar that any detailed reference thereto might be omitted if it were not that renewed emphasis may be laid upon those points which assist the student in arriving at a decision as to the extent of the main parts of the structure; and that an opportunity will be afforded to examine Mozart's general practice. Here it should be pointed out that it is futile to attempt an arbitrary definition of the exact limits of a theme or connecting passage, when the composer has employed the art that conceals art so that one theme melts into another. An endeavour to sever music in this fashion, even mentally, should form no part of the labours of the student of design.

The first subject—which is usually of normal construction, definite tonality and less lengthy than the second subject—ends at the last full or half close before the music begins to modulate. The first subject of the Sonata No. 4, in E flat (last movement) comes to an end at bar nine with a half close in the tonic key. Other examples of subjects ending with an imperfect cadence are to be found in Sonata No. 6, in D (first movement), Sonata No. 13, in B flat (second movement), and No. 16, in C major (first movement).

The bridge passage—that modulatory passage which connects the two subjects—varies considerably in these sonatas: in some it would seem to be detached from the themes on either side of it, and to consist of those scale runs and broken chords which form a type of writing variously known as "conventional passage work" and "padding"; while in others it appears to grow out of and to be a continuation of the thought contained in the subject matter, as in the initial movements of Sonatas Nos. 8 and 13. Further, note the variableness of the length of this connecting portion: in some sonatas it is of a prolonged character (see Sonata No. 15, in F major, first movement); in others, there is practically no bridge passage at all (see Sonata No. 16, in C major, first movement).

The second subject follows in some related key: usually that of the dominant, or in the case of the minor mode, the relative major (see Nos. 8 and 14). The student should refer to the final or recapitulatory section and discover how much of what was previously presented in the dominant key is there transposed to the key of the tonic : this will help him to define the limits of the subject more accurately, although he must remember that on account of its greater length the second subject is liable to curtailment on its reappearance. Frequently there are several sections in this subject (see No. 14, in C minor), which is said to extend to the double bar and repeat, which usually, and with Mozart, so far as the pianoforte sonatas are concerned, invariably mark the end of the exposition : further, throughout these sonatas the various sections of the subjects have but one key as their tonal centre, and the end of the sections is marked by a cadence in that key. The last section of the second subject is frequently detached under the appellation of "concluding section" or "codetta" to the first portion of the movement; but the structure and contents will guide the student as to the most suitable description.

The development or free fantasia section forms the second portion of this threefold design; and herein the themes previously presented are developed or worked out. In Mozart's sonatas this section is frequently episodical in character. Banister says : "The absence of 'working' in certain of Mozart's pianoforte sonatas was not, we may be quite sure, from any lack of power or resource in the greatest writer of his time, but from an absence of pedantry and the untrammelled sense of fitness which characterised him . . . . an instance of his exuberant wealth of melodic resource." This section commences after the double bar occurring at the end of the exposition and extends to the recapitulation or repetition of the first part which usually opens with a complete restatement of the first subject. Very rarely an exception occurs, as in the first movement of Sonata No. 9 in D major, where the *second* subject marks the opening of the recapitulatory section: an example followed by Brahms in his Pianoforte Quintet, Op. 66. The bridge may be altered in length, modified or omitted in this section, as both subjects being in the tonic key there is now no necessity for a passage of a transitional nature. It would not, however, be generally desirable for the two themes to *directly* succeed each other; for the contrast between them—an essential factor—would in such case be forced out of perspective and unduly exaggerated.

The C major Sonata No. 16 provides an interesting departure from the orthodox, for the first subject is recapitulated in the subdominant key and the second subject alone is in the key of the tonic. Again, in Sonata No. 10, first movement, the second subject reappears in the dominant key: and is, of necessity, later amended so as to conclude in the tonic. Examine also the first movement of the Sonata No. 1 in C major where the first subject ending with a full close in the exposition is so varied in the recapitulation as to end with a half close. Occasionally one of the sections of the second subject is omitted and fresh material substituted (see Sonata No. 14 in C minor, first movement). It is interesting also to observe how frequently Mozart concludes the second subject with a prolonged shake on the penultimate chord.

The coda begins at that point where the music departs from the material announced in the exposition. Mozart employed the coda much less frequently than his successors: nor in his time had it assumed the importance with which it is now vested. The most noteworthy example in these sonatas is that attached to the first movement of the C minor Sonata. The repetition of the development and recapitulation would appear to be much more generally employed by Mozart than by Beethoven. It is however difficult to dogmatise, for there is seldom unanimity on the point among the several editions of the sonatas of the earlier master. Beethoven's change may be accepted as a definite artistic advance; but the present day practice of executants in ignoring the repeat marks at the close of the exposition is to be deplored. It would seem to be forgotten that the repetition of the first section was a distinct and valuable educational factor: it familiarised hearers with the subject matter so that they were the better enabled to appreciate the thematic development in the middle section. The presumption that a composer's ideas are more easily assimilated and retained nowadays is delightfully optimistic but hardly justifiable.

THE MIDDLE MOVEMENT.

For his slow movement Mozart made use of many forms, among them:

(1). Simple binary form.

(2). Simple ternary form.

(3). Modified sonata (i.e., without development or middle section) as in the Andantino, Sonata No. 9 in D major.

(4). Unabridged sonata as in the Andante, Sonata No. 15 in F major. When sonata form with development is employed for a middle movement the plan is modified in one or more of the following ways: *(a)* Bridge passage omitted. *(b)* Development short. *(c)* Subjects curtailed in the recapitulation.

(5). Old or simple rondo form as in the Adagio, Sonata No. 14 in C minor. The use of this form for a slow movement is exceedingly rare. Subject is varied on each reappearance. Coda optional.

(6). Another modification of the sonata plan very much employed by Mozart is built in the following form: Part I, subject in tonic key, bridge and second subject in related key. Part II, episode containing some slight allusion or bearing affinity to the subject matter. Part III, repetition of Part I, with both subjects in the tonic key and coda (optional). If:

(1) The above key scheme is employed;

(2) The bridge passage is used;

(3) The two subjects are contrasted;

(4) The episode contains a reference to the thematic material, no matter how slight, for it must be remembered that Mozart's development sections are often episodical;

Then, the term "modified sonata" would seem to be more rational than the much-used description "ternary form" or "binary form," as some older writers would prefer.

THE FINALE.

As a concluding movement, Mozart chose the sonata form, the old rondo form (see Sonatas No. 16 and 17), modern rondo-sonata form and the air with variations.

In regard to the modern rondo-sonata form, which is a fusion of the sonata and rondo principles, Mozart represents the transition stage between the old and new schemes. The established plan is therefore subject to modification: sometimes the sonata principle predominates, as in the last movement of Sonata No. 19, in D major; or again, the idea underlying the rondo is in the ascendancy, as in Sonata No. 15, in F major. Hence the description "MODIFIED rondo-sonata form."

These notes will serve to make clear the sense in which the various terms will be employed in the oncoming analyses. This is desirable; for, unfortunately, there exists considerable divergence in the matter of nomenclature. I have been prompted to point out the numerous exceptions to the general structure as displayed in these sonatas, because students most often fall into error through endeavouring to make the com-

position which they are wishful to analyse conform to
the established order in a rigid, mathematical manner.
The result is disastrous; for they foolishly attempt to
convert the lovely forest of the composer's fancy into
some wretched timber-yard of their own creation!

Now, as a final word of advice before commencing
the detailed analysis of the sonatas, let me urge the
student of musical form to ever seek to obtain a "bird's
eye" view of a musical work.   I would that every page
of printed music set before the student of design could
be marked with a commanding P.T.O.*   Be not afraid
to turn over the pages; for the first sheet may tell all
that it is necessary to know; or again, it may tell
nothing.   Aim at securing a general conception of the
broad outlines before devoting time to the consideration of detail.

---

* In examination papers where questions have been based
upon a binary dance from a Bach or Handel suite, it has been
abundantly evident from the answers that several candidates
have only looked at the first half of the movement. The fact
that the composition (as they saw it) ended in the dominant
key has not, apparently, disturbed what might most fittingly
be described as their *calculations*. This from students seeking
a coveted diploma!

SONATA NO. 1, IN C MAJOR.

SONATA NO. I, IN C MAJOR.

(Zimmermann Edition.)

First movement, "Allegro." Key of C major. Sonata form.

Exposition: bars 1-12^3; first subject, 12^3-6; bridge passage; 16^3-31: 31^1-8; second subject. Development: bars 39-57. Recapitulation: 58-67^3: first subject; 67^4-9^4; bridge passage; 70^1-100; second subject in tonic key.

Second movement, "Andante." Key of F. Ternary form.

Part I: bars 1-29a; Part II, bars 29b-43; Part III, bars 44-75.

Third movement, "Allegro." Key of C. Sonata form.

Exposition: bars 1-11^2; first subject; 11^2-23^1; bridge passage; 23^2-39^1: 39^2-57a. Second subject. Development: bars 57b-87. Recapitulation: 87^2-97^2; first subject. 97^2-109^1; bridge passage; 109^2-59; second subject in tonic key.

FIRST MOVEMENT.

At the opening of the first sonata a point arises the consideration of which may help to place the student in a correct attitude toward analysis of form. The extent of the first subject is a matter of question; for there is little break in the continuity of the music until the half-close is reached at bar 16. One authority has indicated bar 5 as the end of the first principal theme, but it would seem that it is not until bar 6 that the subject begins to "move." Again, the whole of this matter (1-16) has been regarded as first subject ending with a half-close; but, if this be so, why the definite cadence at bar 12? The avoided cadence at bar 10, together with the succeeding material, would point to bar 12 as the end of the subject proper. Bars 13 *et seq*. appear as intermediate matter or bridge passage where the tonic key sense is weakened.

The bridge passage of four bars' duration concludes with a half close in the key of the tonic. Note the repeated use of the chromatic tonic seventh chord. The fact that these bars fail to perform the accepted office of a bridge, i.e., transition to the new key, may have some bearing upon the point of tonality noted in the second theme.

The second subject opens rather curiously on the dominant note of the new key, followed by dominant and tonic harmonies in A minor (bars 17-8), which, being repeated a tone lower, bring us to G major, where a tangible theme is introduced, ending with a full close at bar 31. Further, this unusual opening of the subject seems to indicate a desire on the part of Mozart to depart from the orthodox tonal relationship of the two subjects. This is also apparent in the last movement of Sonata No. 12, and suggested a course which Beethoven was not slow to follow.

The development section suggests rather than employs the matter of both subjects. Opening in G minor, the course of modulation is through D minor, C major, A minor, G minor, F major, C major and G major to the tonic key of C major. It will be noted that Mozart touches the tonic key twice before such use is necessary. The usual rule for a middle section, so far as tonality is concerned, is "any key except the tonic"; but before charging Mozart with weakness in this respect we should reflect that when these sonatas were written it was but a reach of the hand back to the days of the suite, when the tonic key with change of mode was extensively or solely employed.

In the recapitulation the first subject is altered and merges into the bridge passage, which is also shortened. If a definite point for the termination of the subject has to be supplied, then the half close at bar 67 would be most fitting. One would fail to see how such a necessity should arise were it not that some examination papers—but that is another story.

The second subject, duly transposed to the key of the tonic, is extended by the interpolation of some passage work (bars 82 et seq.) which recalls the portion of the bridge previously omitted. Note the curious trans-

ference of the opening of the subject from the third
to the first beat in the bar, and the consequent irregularity when the former accentuation is restored at bar
73; even this restoration is only of a temporary nature,
for the theme which commenced in the exposition at
bar 20 is transferred to the half-bar at 74. There is
no coda proper to the movement—the reiteration of the
cadence chord and slight extension of the phrase serving to heighten the sense of finality.

Second Movement.

The first part consists of two sentences, the first
ending at bar 11 and the second at bar 29 with a perfect cadence in the key of the dominant. Bars 27^1-9
might be regarded as a slight codetta.

The middle section (key, C major) opens in a vein
somewhat akin to the first part—a point which has led
some analysts to regard the movement as a modified
sonata form without a bridge passage. The keys of
G major, D minor and G minor are passed through
before the original tonic key is reached.

The first part is repeated with such modifications
as are necessary that the two sentences may end in the
tonic key of F. The first sentence is slightly curtailed, while the second is extended with coda-like
effect. Although the reiterated crotchet notes (bar 44)
have been declared as the opening of the Da Capo
portion the music really anticipates this somewhat; for
the middle section ends with the half close at bar 42
and the melodic run which follows leans toward the

succeeding matter. Too often students and also writers on musical form ignore such passages : the performer cannot do so. Difficult as it may sometimes be to decide the point as to whether these phrases are supplementary or introductory in character, they cannot be left, as it were, lying about—a kind of "nobody's child"; nor, if there is to be any life or progression in music, can they go off in meteor fashion into space.

FINALE.

The first subject extends to bar 11^2 and ends with a perfect cadence. The fore phrase is one of four bars duration : and the after-phrase is extended to six bars.

The bridge passage is conventional passage writing, and after establishing the key of G major moves to D major, and returning to the dominant ends with a half close.

The second subject consists of two sections—the first a sixteen-bar phrase beginning and ending in the dominant key, is strongly contrasted in character with the first theme, and is constructed almost entirely on the initial motive. The student may think that the portion indicated as second section of the second subject (39-57) is overlong, and that there are breaks in the continuity of the movement later; but, if he will follow this latter portion, either mentally or at the instrument, he will perceive that from 39^2 the leaning is all toward the final chord, while the harmonic basis remains the same throughout, viz., the cadential harmonies so frequently employed by the master: supertonic, dominant and tonic.

The initial figures of both subjects are inverted and embellished in the "working out" section, in conjunction with modulation. Opening with the second subject in G major, the music passes through E minor and A minor. The first subject then appears, first in E minor and again in D minor, forming a descending sequence proceeding to the opening notes of the phrase as it would appear in C major, when the course of the theme is arrested. It would appear as if the composer thought the return to the original theme in the original key almost too subtle. The interruption undoubtedly grips the attention and lends emphasis to the opening of the recapitulatory section. The psychological insight of Mozart was really great.

The recapitulation is regular. At bar 133 the cadence, weakened and extended, resolves itself into a half-close. The opening theme of the second subject is then taken directly and by inversion forming a stretto-like passage. Following on this, the matter of the second section is proceeded with at bar 149, thence onwards to the end being a transposition of the closing bars of the enunciation section with reiterated cadence.

SONATA NO. 2, IN F MAJOR.

SONATA NO. 2, IN F MAJOR.
(*Zimmermann Edition.*)

First movement, "Assai Allegro." Key of F. Sonata form.

Exposition: bars 1-13^1; first subject. 13^1-26^2. Bridge passage. 27-43^1, 43^2-56; second subject. Development: 57-82. Recapitulation: 83-95; first subject. 95-108; bridge passage. 109-44. Second subject in tonic key.

Second movement, "Adagio." Key of F minor. Ternary form. Part I, 1-24; Part II, 25-32; Part III, 33-60.

Third movement, "Presto." Key of F. Sonata form. Exposition: bars 1-17^2; first subject. 17^3-38; bridge passage. 39-67^1; 67^2-78^2; second subject. Developments: 78-107. Recapitulation: 108^3-124^2; first subject. 124-49; bridge passage. 150-78; 178^3-91. Second subject in tonic key.

FIRST MOVEMENT.

The first subject is of somewhat irregular construction : the fore phrase of four bars' duration is of a definite, if undistinguished, character, but in the respon-

sive phrase which is extended by a repetition of bar 5
and, later, bars 7-9, Mozart seems to be chiefly en-
gaged in avoiding a full close; and this without the
employment of either great ingenuity or artistry.

The second subject is in the usual dominant key.
Some theorists SEE a resemblance between this and
the first theme; for it commences with the opening
notes of the first subject (see the bass of bars 1-2)
taken by inverse movement. This surely is one of
those tremendously subtle points—so ordinary as to be
quite accidental—the making of which has brought the
analyst and his work into derision. The touchstone
is this: is such "thematic development" heard in performance, even after the listener has been informed of
its presence in the music: and if so, is the result really
worth the aural energy expended? The matter is only
referred to here because of the opportunity which is
afforded of emphasising the fact that the art of music
makes its appeal through the ear, not the eye.

The development is rather episodical in character,
and opening in C major passes through the key of D
minor to F major. The bold opening of the second
subject booms out several times and the passage to
the recapitulatory section is insinuatingly effected
through the use of a figure derived (bar 5) from the
first subject.

In the recapitulation the only departure from the
exposition, other than that of tonality, is the additional reference to the opening motive at bar 117.

SECOND MOVEMENT.

This, in every way the most interesting moment in the sonata, is the type of movement which Prout would have described as binary in form; and it naturally falls into three parts.

The first part consists of two sentences, the first, one of eight bars, in the key of F minor; and the second in the relative key of A flat major, comes to an end at bar 21, the succeeding matter being in the nature of a codetta. The second part has reference to both sentences, and leads from B flat minor to C minor, in which key it ends with a half close.

The repetition of the first part has been placed at bar 33, where the first theme reappears in C minor; but as the music later, at bar 37, is identical with the opening of the movement, there is perhaps need of explanation. *Why place the opening of Part III at bar 32 in preference to bar 37?* Because (1) the half cadence at bar 32 is very definite, and it is extremely doubtful if Mozart would make so pronounced a break in the continuity of the music without full appreciation of, and definite intention as to, the effect. (2) The phrase opening at bar 37 strikes the ear (which is the final court of appeal) as being a responsive phrase to that announced at bar 33. Play it over and listen carefully.

FINALE.

Only two points call for further comment in this movement.

The development section opens with the second subject matter (bars 79-86), and being repeated sequentially (bars 87-94), the original key of ·F major is reached; but a variation of the concluding bars quickly leads to D minor, on the dominant harmony of which key the section ends. The recapitulation opens strikingly on C natural, suggesting the capricious element with which Mozart infected so many of his concluding movements.

As in the exposition, the concluding section of the movement is merely cadential in character. Four bars (188-91) are added, but although they naturally add to the conclusiveness, they can scarcely be described as coda; for they are formed only by prolonging the final tonic harmony.

SONATA NO. 3, IN B FLAT MAJOR.

SONATA NO. 3, IN B FLAT MAJOR.
(Zimmermann Edition.)

First movement, "Allegro Moderato." Key, B flat. Form, sonata.

Exposition: 1-8^1, first subject; 8^2-17^1, bridge passage; 17-34, 34-40, second subject. Development: 41-69. Recapitulation: 70-7, first subject; 77^2-86^1, bridge passage; 86-103, 103-9, second subject in tonic.

Second movement, "Andante Amoroso." Key, E flat. Form, sonata.

Exposition: 1-15^1, first subject; 16^1-28^1, bridge passage; 28-43, 43-6, second subject. Development: 47-58. Recapitulation: 59-72, first subject; 72-3, transition; 74-88, bridge passage; 88^2-106, second subject in tonic.

Third movement, "Allegro." Key, B flat. Form, rondo-sonata.

Exposition: 1-18^2, principal subject; 19-28, bridge passage; 29-40, second subject; 40-4, link; 44-52, principal subject. Episode: 53-71. Recapitulation: 72-89, principal subject; 89^2-90^1, transition; 91-124,

bridge passage; 125-37, second subject in tonic; 137^1-
43^1, link; 143-60, principal subject; 160^2-3, coda.

FIRST MOVEMENT.

There is nothing in the plan of this movement call-
ing for special comment.

SECOND MOVEMENT.

To a certain extent this little movement reflects the
atmosphere of stilted formality which characterised
the eighteenth century; and yet the music can only
be described as unpretentious and refreshing. Within
these two short pages many points may be observed
which rival in charm of outline and wealth of detail
some quaint and delightfully irregular example of
the potter's art.

It has previously been noted that when full sonata
form is used for a middle movement the development
section is usually quite brief. Here is an example.
Although the section could not be said to contain new
matter, it is evident that no serious thought has de-
tained the composer on his journey back to the original key.

The treatment of the first subject on its reappearance by the use of the triplet figure which suggests
the second subject is sufficiently interesting to be noted.
This ornamentation appears to be something in the
nature of an "amende" for the poverty of the middle
section; and the unusual tonality of the bridge passage might be likewise regarded.

The two chords of E flat major which in the exposition served to emphasise the end of the first subject now contain a D flat, and so introduce the bridge in the key of the subdominant (A flat). Passing through F minor, the music leads by means of a half-close to the second subject transposed to the tonic key.

THIRD MOVEMENT.

This is a great movement—one that is calculated to put to confusion those who declare that the modern rondo-sonata form had its origin in Beethoven. It may appear to modern ears to be somewhat thin in texture and lacking the brilliance which dazzles; but with those points we are not now concerned. What is material is this : that in such a movement Mozart has enunciated plans and principles which, consolidated by later composers, have formed an established art-form.

The principal subject contains two phrases, the responsive phrase being extended by a repetition of bars 13-4. Bars 40-4 form a link oscillating between the keys of the dominant and tonic, and concluding with a short cadenza. These bars might be regarded as a part of the second subject matter; and the peculiar driving rhythm produced by the trill on the second beat certainly creates a cadential effect which supports this view : in that case the *ad lib.* passage would be the link. *A deeper analysis, however, might reveal to us a purpose on the part of the composer to weaken the key sense from bar 40, in which case these*

bars are intermediate matter leading to the restate-
ment of the principal theme. Although only the first
eight bars of the subject (the purely melodic section)
are represented, they adequately convey the recapitulatory idea. It is in such touches that the master hand
is manifested.

The episode in the relative minor key of G is of
simple binary construction. Bars 69-71 are a retransition to the key of B flat major. This change is so
charmingly executed that it may be of interest to examine the harmonic progression. Following the G
minor chord with which the episode ends, at bar 69
an inverted minor ninth is employed. Viewed from
G minor it is a chromatic ninth on the tonic, but as a
dominant ninth it leads to the chord of C major.
Treating this chord as subdominant harmony in G, it
serves to introduce the chord known as the augmented
sixth in that key, which duly resolves upon dominant
harmony. Again, regarding this latter chord as subdominant harmony, the chord in bar 71 may be taken
as an inversion of the augmented sixth in A major,
and the D sharp being then E flat the chord becomes
a dominant seventh in the original key of B flat.
Throughout this lengthy attempt at explanation (for
I am quite prepared to hear that I am all wrong, and
that I must be very old-fashioned to talk of augmented sixths and false notation) and despite the
employment of the cumbersome terms with which the
beautiful art of music is saddled, we must not forget
that we were prompted to such detailed and technical

examination by the charm with which the music had
melted from one kev to another: nor must we forget
that two things are necessary to a full appreciation:
a knowledge of facts and a susceptibility to charm.
The first acquirement must not be permitted to rob us
of the second possession. Play these few bars over
again, and if you say that they are simple, remember
that you at once admit one of the qualities of beauty;
for Emerson states that we ascribe beauty to that
which is simple; which has no superfluous parts; which
exactly answers its end. This retransition possesses
all three qualities.

Perhaps students of form may take a lesson from
the renewed controversy on the methods of explaining
harmonic combinations, and the lesson, which is two-
fold, is this: that *terms* do not matter; but that terms,
for certain purposes, are necessary, and if they suc-
cessfully conjure up a mental or aural vision of the
THING, then any name suffices. Let me elaborate. A
chemist may, by the exercise of his sense of taste or
smell, or the employment of some process, discover
the nature of the contents of every bottle on his store
shelves: but the association of some name with a particular drug enables him to place a label upon the
bottle and so facilitate matters in innumerable ways.
The fact that a label is affixed to the bottle, or that
the name is neither euphonious nor rational does not
necessarily imply that he is ignorant of the nature and
effect of the contents. Should he personally disap-
prove of the name given to a certain article, it would

be futile for him to substitute one more to his liking unless it possessed qualities sufficiently marked to break down custom and tradition so that purchasers employ his term in preference to that hitherto in general use. Now, in music, we have labels; and there is no reason why a reference to "augmented sixths" and "false notation" should arouse the wrath of the most perfect musician. That explanations may be simplified is perfectly true; but if the old term is to be superseded then the necessity arises for the provision of a rational term which must not fail in exactness of meaning or clearness of definition. It is one thing to say, pointing to a certain chord, that it is the first inversion of the subdominant harmony with the root and third chromatically altered, and that such chromatic alterations are indeed chromatic passing notes; but it is another thing to coin a short term which will convey those points adequately. Now the older and much-abhorred term "augmented sixth" has come to mean something definite, not perhaps because of its fitness, but by reason of the association. Similarly, too, in musical analysis, there is no reason why the terms "first subject," "second subject" and "bridge passage" should distress the musical soul. Every composition contains a principal theme; one or more secondary themes and some connecting matter. It is the duty of every executant to be acquainted with these themes, their relative importance and extent; and it is also necessary to have terms attached to them for reference. The terms hitherto and still employed fulfil their purpose admirably. The "thing" and its effect are the points that are vital : the name is an accident —sometimes unfortunate, I readily admit; but just as the label on the bottle does not necessarily leave the chemist ignorant, so the labelling of music need not and should not weaken true appreciation.

The bridge passage in the recapitulation is quite different to that employed in the exposition. Opening in E flat major, the music passes through C minor and (over an inverted and direct dominant pedal) introduces the principal theme. The use of this fresh material for the bridge suggests a leaning to the episodical element of the rondo form, while the additional reference to the first subject might be regarded in the same light; or again, the use of the subject in this manner may indicate that Mozart, like his successor, was not content with the middle section being entirely episodical in character, feeling that it should approximate more closely to the development section of the sonata form. The fact that such use occurs in what is obviously the final portion of the movement in this instance is immaterial; but it is important to note that it suggested a mode of treatment which later became general.

After the return of the second subject, transposed to the tonic key, the principal subject is given complete, and a short codetta based on the last three notes of the subject emphasises the cadence.

SONATA NO. 4, IN E FLAT MAJOR.

SONATA NO. 4, IN E FLAT MAJOR.

(Zimmermann Edition.)

First movement, "Adagio." Key, E flat. Form, binary. Part I, 1-15; Part II, 16-33; coda, 34-6.

Second movement. Keys, B flat and E flat. Form, ternary.

Minuetto I. 1^3-13, subject; 13^3-9^2, digression; 19^3-31^2, subject; 31-3, coda. Minuetto II. 1-17^2, subject; 17^3-25^1, digression; 25-41, subject. Minuetto I, Da Capo.

Third movement, "Allegro." Key, E flat. Form, sonata.

Exposition: 1-9, first subject; 9-16, bridge passage; 16^2-36, 36-40 *(a)*, second subject. Development: 40 *(b)*-62. Recapitulation, 62^2-70, first subject; 10-7, bridge passage; 77-97, 97-103, second subject in tonic.

First Movement.

This sonata, together with No. 11, in A major, provides the only examples in these sonatas of an opening movement in any form other than sonata form;

and even this movement might be regarded as representing that form in its embryonic stage while yet the binary principle predominated. The first part consists of two sections: the fore section ends at bar 8 where the double dominant key of F major is reached; and the after sentence ends at bar 15 with a full close in the dominant key, B flat major. A link leads to the repetition.

In Part II the first section is repeated, considerably modified, and extends to eleven bars: the second section is given as in Part I, transposed to the tonic key. The codetta is based upon the opening theme.

Second Movement.

The minuettos are ternary in construction, regarded either separately or as a whole.

Minuetto I.

The first section ends at bar 13. There is a fore phrase of four bars ending in tonic, but the responsive phrase is extended by repetition and codetta, and ends in the key of the dominant.

Some modulatory chords (bars 13^3-9^2) afford relief and lead back to the tonic key by means of a half-close).

The first part is repeated at bars 19-31 and so modified as to end in tonic key. It does not need the eye of a microscope to see that the theme is transferred to the bass, and it may be questioned why so obvious a point should be noted; but so many pianoforte students rush past such milestones without themselves recognising their existence, much less their import, that the fate of those whom they are wishful to carry along with them is exceedingly unenviable.

This is just the type of movement which would serve to make young players acquainted with the principles of design. Too often "musical form" is considered to be a most advanced study—one of those *extra* subjects which may be relegated to the to-morrow which never comes; and if this study be so delayed, a difficulty is created, for the performer's fingers are concerning themselves with involved designs whilst he is incapable of appreciating the simplest structure. Let "form" or "design" be noted as early as possible; for the child is simply longing for that little talk which will put his various wonderful but unmarshalled thoughts into useful order. When the child has discovered for himself the fact that he has not to learn the last pages of a particular composition because they are the same as the opening bars, he has proved the capacity of the child-mind for imbibing the broad principles of construction.

Minuetto II.

The first portion of the trio consists of two sections of eight bars in tonic and dominant keys respectively.

The middle section is quite contrasted in character, and concludes with a foreshadowing of the first part, which is then repeated with both sentences in the key of the tonic.

It should be noted that the form of this second minuetto (theme one in tonic, theme two in dominant: digression: themes one and two both in tonic) represents a stage in the transition from the simple binary to the modern sonata form.

THIRD MOVEMENT.

In this movement the bridge passage is entirely in the key of the *dominant*, concluding with a half-close in that key at bar 16—a fact which has led some theorists to regard this portion as the opening section of the second subject.

The second subject of quite contrasted character enters without formality in the dominant key. The matter of the first subject is used throughout the short development section; and the keys employed are F minor, E flat major, A flat major, B flat minor and C minor. The student should examine the means by which Mozart effects these transitions.

SONATA NO. 5, IN G MAJOR.

SONATA NO. 5, IN G MAJOR.
(*Zimmermann Edition.*)

First movement, "Allegro." Key, G. Form, sonata.

Exposition: bars 1-17, first subject; 17-23, bridge passage; 24-44, 44-54 *(a)*, second subject. Development: 54 *(b)*-72. Recapitulation: 72-84, first subject; 84-90, bridge passage: 91-121, second subject in tonic key.

Second movement, "Andante." Key, C. Form, modified sonata.

Exposition: bars 1-4, first subject; 5-8, bridge passage; 9-14, second subject. Development: 14 *(b)*-23 Recapitulation: 23^2-7, first subject; 28-31, bridge passage; 32-7, second subject in tonic key; 37 *(b)*-9, codetta.

Third movement, "Presto." Key, G. Form, sonata.

Exposition: bars 1-24^2, first subject; 24^3-40, bridge passage; 41-73, 73-97, 97-102, second subject. Development: 103-70. Recapitulation: 172-95, first subject; 195-211, bridge passage; 212-77, second subject in tonic key.

First Movement.

This is neither a very full nor very equal movement. The music of the exposition breaks itself up in obvious fashion, while of the free fantasia section, to say that the matter is different from the first portion is perhaps all that one could say—it might be unkind to add that it should not be so. A most instructive and interesting point occurs in the recapitulation. Only the first four bars of the first subject are exactly represented, and they are repeated sequentially in the key of A minor, after which four new bars are added to complete the phrase. Beethoven has made extensive use of this device hinted at by Mozart: and with striking results. One of the most notable examples is the Sonata No. 17, in D minor. It is but natural, however, with all the advantages of close upon one hundred and fifty years' growth and development, that we should feel that the early master failed by reason of pulling in his horse just as he was about to leap.

Second Movement.

The first theme is really an eight-bar sentence, the position of the cadences indicating that the time signature would more properly have been $\frac{2}{4}$. Such errors are of frequent occurrence in the works of the great masters. Prout says this simply arises from inattention on the part of composers who are often indifferent, so long as the cadence comes on an accent, whether that accent is strong or weak.

It is of particular interest, in view of the above references and quotation, to note that the barring of the theme is altered in the middle section so that the cadence chord falls on the main accent of the bar. The recapitulation opens with a short chromatic passage prefacing the first subject which is altered, and through dominant harmony leads to the bridge passage in the key of the subdominant. After opening in F major, the bridge passage quickly moves to the tonic and leads to the second subject through a half close in that key. The presentation of the bridge passage in a new key was noted in the middle movement of the previous sonata; and would appear to be employed as a means of quickening the interest in a movement where the middle section is lacking the requisite development or contrast. Such points are invaluable as a manifestation of the perfect sense of proportion and fitness possessed by the composer. The coda is based upon the first subject. A delightful freshness is produced by the change in the harmony accompanying the theme.

FINALE.

The first subject opens with so joyous a lilt as to lead one to suppose the movement to be a rondo. The first section of eight bars' duration over a reiterated tonic pedal point is both regular and tangible; but the responsive section is more discoursive and extended by many repetitions, ends at bar 24[2] with a perfect cadence. There is no marked break in the music at this point, for the retardation over the tonic harmony weakens the effectiveness of the cadence. The character of the succeeding bars, however, with their restless vacillating harmonic swing, stamps the portion commencing at bar 24 ^{3}, and extending to bar 40 as supplementary matter; and as it, moreover, serves to introduce the new key, there seems no possible objection to the description "bridge passage," while, on the other hand, one would be prepared to readily admit the feasibility of an analysis which suggested bar 40 as the end of the first subject. Two important sentences and a short codetta-like phrase combine to make the second subject matter.

The development section is founded upon the second subject repeated in various keys. It displays marked power and intensity of feeling, and provides a complete answer to those who aver that Mozart lacked the dramatic instinct. The middle section comes to a close at bar 138 in the relative key of E minor, and is followed by the codetta to the exposition in that key. The sequential chords of retransition—whatever their weakness or strength to modern ears—must surely have been regarded as daring in the time of Mozart.

The recapitulatory section is quite regular. The concluding bars (see the cadence before the repeat, bar 272) are altered. Mozart was quick to see the necessity for this adjustment, so that the sense of finality might be weakened and the ear thus prepared for the repetition of the development and recapitulatory sections. A simple, perfect cadence is added after the repeat.

SONATA NO. 6, IN D MAJOR.

SONATA NO. 6, IN D MAJOR.

(Zimmermann Edition.)

First movement, "Allegro." Key, D. Form, sonata.

Exposition: 1-9, or 17, first subject; 9 or 17-21, bridge passage; 22-44, 44-51, second subject. Development, 52-71. Recapitulation: 72-80 or 88, first subject; 80 or 88-92, bridge passage; 93-127, second subject in tonic key.

Second movement, "Andante." Key, A. Form, ternary.

Part I: 1-16, subject; 17-30, digression; 31-46, subject. Part II: 46^3-69. Part III: 70-92.

Third movement, "Andante." Key, D. Form, air with variations.

FIRST MOVEMENT.

The conclusion of the recapitulation differs from that of the exposition. It is, however, doubtful if any portion could be regarded as coda; for the new matter is in the nature of an interpolation (bar 119) rather than an addition.

SECOND MOVEMENT.

This is a somewhat irregularly conceived movement. Note the changed tonality of the sentence of digression and the embellishment of the theme.

FINALE.

As a constituent part of the pianoforte sonata Mozart only employs this form twice. The theme is presented in a very square form; but is clearly ternary in conception: bars 1-9 provide the first section ending in D major. A new sentence opens at bar 9 *(b) and the reappearance of the opening theme at bar 14 reveals the ternary basis.* The variations do not call for comment.

SONATA NO. 7, IN C MAJOR.

SONATA NO. 7, IN C MAJOR.

(Zimmermann Edition.)

First movement, "Allegro con Spirito." Key C. Form, sonata.

Exposition: 1-21, first subject; 21-31, bridge passage; 32-54, 54-8, second subject. Development: 59-93. Recapitulation: 94-116, first subject; 116-26, bridge passage; 127-48, 148-52, 152-55, second subject in tonic key.

Second movement, "Andante quasi Adagio." Key, F major. Form, ternary.

Part I: bars 1-32. Part II: 33-44. Part III: 45-76, 76-9, coda.

Third movement, "Allegretto Grazioso." Key, C. Form, modified rondo-sonata.

Exposition: 1-20, principal subject; 20-40, bridge passage; 40^2-78, second subject in dominant; 78^2-93^2, link or retransition; 93-109, principal subject; 109-16, link episode; 117-43, recapitulation; 143^2-89, second subject in tonic; 189-208, principal subject; 208-53, coda.

First Movement.

The close at the end of the bridge passage gives the effect of a double dominant, and so the bars 33-4 are rendered necessary before the introduction of the second subject.

The characteristic unisonal opening of the theme is used in the middle section. This is, perhaps, the first example so far reached in the sonatas where there is a definite thematic development. In the recapitulation of the first subject there is an additional reference to the first subject, but in the minor mode. while the concluding section makes further use of the same matter.

Finale.

A departure from the accepted plan should be noted in that the third part opens with the *second* subject. One can imagine that in the early days of the use of the rondo-sonata form such employment of the second theme served to emphasise its presence in the scheme of things. Perhaps, too, Mozart felt that a complete résumé of the first part would have dwarfed the middle part. The restatement of the first subject would have satisfied; but might only have increased the lack of proportion. The presentation of the second theme and a conclusion with the main theme was a happy solution of a real difficulty.

SONATA NO. 8, IN A MINOR.

SONATA NO. 8, IN A MINOR.
(Zimmermann Edition.)

First movement, "Allegro Maestoso." Key, A minor. Form, sonata.

Exposition: 1-9, first subject; 9-22, bridge passage; 22-45, 45-9, second subject in relative major. Development: 50-79. Recapitulation: 79-88, first subject; 88-103, bridge passage; 103-33, second subject in tonic (minor mode).

Second movement, "Andante Cantabile." Key, F major. Form, ternary.

Part I: 1-32. Part II: 32-54^2. Part III: 54^3-87. Or (as modified sonata form).

Exposition: 1-9, first subject; 9-15, bridge passage; 16-30, 30-2, second subject. Development: 32^3-54^2. Recapitulation: 54-62, first subject; 62-8, bridge passage; 69-85, 85-7, second subject in tonic key.

Third movement, "Presto." Key, A minor. Form, modified rondo-sonata.

Exposition: 1-20, principal subject; 21-8, bridge passage; 29-87, second subject; 87-106, link; 107-24, principal subject; 124-42, coda. Episode: 142-74. Recapitulation: 174-94, principal subject; 194-202, bridge passage; 203-45, second subject; 245-52, coda.

FIRST MOVEMENT.

The first subject is a straightforward eight-bar sentence ending with a full close. It is an example of the purity of tonality observable in subjects in the minor mode by the great masters. The conclusion of the subject and the opening of the bridge passage provide an example of overlapping phrases.

The bridge passage grows out of the main theme and modulates to C minor, ending with an imperfect cadence. A similar employment of the minor mode previous to the entry of a subject in the major key will also be found in Sonata No. 12. Such a procedure lends an added freshness to the theme.

According to the definition by which we have bound ourselves in previous words there are three sections in the second subject, but the concluding section (45-9) is founded upon the opening theme, and is just the type of concluding phrase which may most happily be referred to as "codetta."

The development section opens with the principal subject in C major; but a diversion is effected at bar 53 seemingly according to the notation, to the key of F. Here, however, occurs a somewhat anomalous oscillation, for at bar 55 the D flat (minor ninth to C, the dominant of F) is enharmonically changed and seems to indicate a transition to D minor. Instead of resolving on that harmony, however, a return is immediately made to the dominant harmony of F, rendering quite nugatory and inexplicable the previous enharmonic change. Still, I suppose a composer is entitled to change his mind! Most beautifully this dominant seventh in F (bar 56) becomes an augmented sixth chord in the key of E minor, and the remainder of this part consists mainly of working founded on the first subject passing through the keys of E minor, A minor, D minor and C major back to A minor. Note the use of the ornamented pedal bass from bar 58 onward: the tonic pedal in E leading as dominant to A minor: from tonic of A minor as dominant to D minor and so on.

The chromatic run leading to the first subject opens the recapitulatory portion.

The bridge passage begins somewhat differently with an allusion to the first theme in the bass, and the second subject is represented in the minor mode of the tonic.

SECOND MOVEMENT.

It will be noted that two plans are given: in both, of course, the main divisions are the same.

The first part consists of a theme (first subject) of a regular eight-bar construction ending in the tonic key. Following comes a transition or bridge passage (9-16) leading to a half close. At bar 17 a new theme (second subject) is introduced in the key of the dominant, concluding at bar 30. A codetta of two bars' duration completes the first part (exposition).

The middle part begins with the first theme in C major: although episodical in character, the introduction of the subject matter must not be overlooked. The first part is recapitulated entirely in the tonic key.

THIRD MOVEMENT.

The principal subject consists of a fore phrase of eight bars with a half close, and an after phrase extended to twelve bars. At bar 16 an interrupted cadence is formed and bars 12-6 are then repeated, ending with a full close in tonic key. Mozart's rondo subjects are, as a rule, very regular in construction; and any deviation from the normal structure, as in this instance, is caused by a repetition which serves to impress the theme upon the memory.

The secondary theme opens in the unusual key of the mediant minor, and bears what Prout would call a "family likeness" to the first subject. Opening in this key of C minor, the music quickly changes to the major mode, and it would at first appear that the composer sought to establish that key: but the false cadence at bar 52 (repeated at bar 56) banishes the relative major key, and we are led by way of a sequence to the key of E minor. A link which seems to be evolved from the subject matter leads promptly back to A minor. It is somewhat contrapuntal in nature. The episode is in the major mode, and is binary in construction. The tonality rather than the

matter affords relief.   In the recapitulation the second
theme is reduced to its simple sixteen-bar form.   There
is no further repetition of the principal theme.   Very
possibly Mozart had by this time fully recognised the
likeness between the subjects and felt that such curtailment was desirable.

SONATA NO. 9, IN D MAJOR.

SONATA NO. 9, IN D MAJOR.

(Zimmermann Edition.)

First movement, "Allegro con Spirito." Key, D major. Form, sonata.

Exposition: bars 1-7, first subject; 7-16, bridge passage, 16^4-36, 36-9, second subject. Development: 40-78. Recapitulation: 78^4-99, second subject in tonic key; 99-105, first subject; 105^1-112, coda.

Second movement, "Andante con Expressione." Key, G. Form, modified sonata.

Exposition: 1-12^1, first subject; 12-6, bridge passage; 16-38^1, second subject. Development: none. Recapitulation: 38^1-50, first subject; 50-2, bridge passage; 52-74, second subject, 74-93, coda.

Third movement, "Allegro." Key, D major. Form, rondo-sonata.

Exposition: 1-27, principal subject; 27-41, bridge passage; 42-80, second subject; 80-6, link; 87-103, principal subject; 103-9, modulating passage. Episode: 120-74. Recapitulation: 174-90; principal subject, 190-206; bridge passage, 207-45; second subject, 245-9; link, 249-67; principal subject, 267-70. Coda.

First Movement.

The first subject extends to seven bars, being indeed
an eight-bar phrase contracted by an overlapping or
elision at the fourth bar. The key of the tonic is not
quitted throughout the bridge passage, which ends on
dominant harmony at bar 16. Regarding this bridge,
Professor W. H. Hadow says: The first four bars are
melodious enough : and even the rest, though it draws
up and presents arms with the usual eighteenth century
ceremony, has a real touch of life underneath its trap-
pings.*

The bars 38-9 are important. The development section opens with an imitational echo of these two bars :
indeed they permeate the whole section, and with the
bridge and second subject provide the material. Commencing in E minor, the music proceeds sequentially
to D major and thence through B minor and G major
to D major.

The recapitulatory section is particularly noteworthy
because it opens with the *second* subject. This interesting departure from the orthodox plan is also followed in the master's violin sonata in the same key.
The entrance of the subject is here heralded by the
use of the bridge and the repeated dominant chords—
the passage which "draws up and presents arms." This
suggests that in the middle section Mozart uncon-
sciously wandered on to the bridge passage, and ad-

---

* " Sonata Form," **W. H. Hadow.**

hering to it *too* closely, led the ear to expect the second theme: it should be noted that the bridge is not later employed. Supposing such introduction of the second subject not to have been previously intentioned by the master, it gives evidence of great adaptability and courage; and lest the reversal of the usual order of subjects should prove disturbing to the hearer and result in a weakening of the total conclusiveness, Mozart closes the movement with the last section of the second theme. It is a happy and cohesive touch.

Second Movement.

The first theme extends to bar 12 (at bar 11 a double bar and repeat occurs, and the length of the subject is therefore twenty bars). The bridge passage is short and the second subject follows in the usual key. After the dominant harmony at bar 24, there is a reminiscence of the first subject.

There is no development, but a short chromatic phrase leans toward the retrospective section. The coda embodies an embellishment of the first theme and suggests a rondo movement, particularly when regarded in conjunction with the matter at bar 24.

Third Movement.

The main theme (bars 1-17) is a delightful rondo subject—absolutely regular in construction and perfectly spontaneous: indeed, so joyous is the lilt throughout that one is scarcely disposed to spend time upon the examination of details, but the unusual treatment of the passing note (B) in the melody at bars 22 and 24 should be noticed: also the point of imitation with which the second subject opens. This second theme comes to a close at bar 80. The immediately succeeding matter appears at first to be "codetta" to the subject, but the subsequent course changes its character into that of a link or retransition. Following the return of the principal theme there occurs a short modulatory passage based on the conclusion of the supplementary matter to the first subject (the four chords of bars 25-7) and leading to the episode proper. This modulation (which echoes the harmonies in E minor and D major followed by a similar phrase leading to B minor) is most delightfully planned. The reminiscent character of the music covers the marked reduction in movement; and this "measured tread" provides, in turn, a transition, both musically and psychologically subtle, to the section of contrast. The episode in B minor has a marked and recurring tendency toward G major. The keys of E minor, D major and A major are employed, ending in an extended "cadenza." The recapitulation opens with the restatement of the main part of the principal subject, but after the secondary theme is given in the tonic key, the principal subject is finally presented in its complete form. The last four bars are repeated (varied) and the cadence chord extended.

SONATA NO. 10, IN C MAJOR.

SONATA NO. 10, IN C MAJOR.
(Zimmermann Edition.)

First movement, "Allegro Moderato." Key C. Form, sonata.

Exposition: bars 1-12 or 18; first subject, 19-34, 34-42, 42-54, 54-8; second subject. Development: 59-87. Recapitulation: 88-105; first subject, 106-45; second subject in tonic; 145-51, coda.

Second movement, "Andante Cantabile." Key, F. Form, ternary.

Part I: bars 1-21 *(a)*. Part II: 2-21 *(b)*-37 *(a)*: 37 *(b)*-41. Part III: 41-61. Coda, 61-5.

Third movement, "Allegretto." Key, C. Form, sonata.

Exposition: bars 1-20; first subject, 21-32, bridge passage; 33-61, 61-8, second subject. Development: 69-95. Recapitulation: 96-115; first subject, 116-31; bridge passage, 131-64; second subject in tonic key; 164-71, coda.

FIRST MOVEMENT.

This is a thin movement—melodically it is not engaging and harmonically it is rather barren, so once again (but for very different reasons) one is not dis-

posed to devote time to the consideration of detail.
One thought, however, encourages us to a more careful
analysis, and it is this: that in many ways this chatter
of Mozart is not more idle than much new music; while
the fact that it is couched in simple, almost mean,
language rather than the high-sounding, and often-
times little-meaning phraseology of modern creative
technique is apt to soften our judgment. There is a
charm about a Cinderella in her rags and tatters which
is lost to many when the same maiden is bedecked in
the gorgeous attire of the ballroom.

The structure of the movement is curious; but we
may derive instruction from its weaknesses. The remarks regarding the opening of Sonata No. 1 apply
with much force to the first eighteen bars. There is
a perfect cadence at bar 12 and again at bars 14 and
16 with a half-close at bar 18. Any of these points
might be regarded as the end of the subject matter.
Immediately following is a theme in G major, obviously the second subject, but the tonality of the first
section is not by any means well defined. The middle
section is really an episode or transition, rather than
a "working out" of the subject matter. In this connection Banister has already been quoted. Prout says:
"With Mozart's movements in general there is more
episode and less thematic treatment than with either
Haydn or Beethoven. . . . . Clearly it was choice not
inability that caused him in so many instances to prefer the more episodical style." Such apologies point

to a weakness, and the most ardent admirer of Mozart cannot gainsay the fact that in many ways the poverty or episodical style of the development section creates a feeling of incompleteness, if not indeed dissatisfaction. This feeling is intensified when the recapitulatory section is reached; for there has not been sufficient digression to make the return of the subject matter either welcome or grateful. It is surprising that the composer did not appreciate this point: otherwise his architectural sense is perfect.

At bar 106 another irregularity is to be noted. The second subject appears as in the exposition section, in the key of the dominant: it is, however, soon subject to amendment which restores the tonic key.

SECOND MOVEMENT.

Here is simple music of wondrous beauty which will not only compensate for the poverty of the preceding or succeeding movement, but will provide comfort and consolation for all who travel the rough and rugged road of life. After listening to these two pages of sheer music one would be disinclined to question or examine the structural plan did not the words of Robert Schumann come to mind: "Only when the form becomes clear to you will the spirit become so too." Examine then the plan of the movement, and play it over again and again until the understanding is perfect; for this is a movement which we will never outgrow.

SONATA NO. 11, IN A MAJOR.

SONATA NO. 11, IN A MAJOR.
(*Zimmermann Edition.*)

First movement, "Andante Grazioso." Key, A major. Form, variations.

Second movement, minuetto and trio. Form ternary.

Minuetto, key, A major, 1-18; 19-30; 31-48. Trio, key, D major, 1-16; 17-36; 37-52.

Third movement, "Allegretto." Key, A major. Form, ternary.

Part I, 1-25 *(a)*; Part II, 25 *(b)*-65 *(a)*; Part III, 65 *(b)*-89, 89-128.

FIRST MOVEMENT.

This is the only instance in the pianoforte sonatas where Mozart opens with the variation form; and as there is no movement in the sonata written in sonata or first movement form it provides a parallel case to that found in Beethoven's Sonata in A flat, Op. 26.

Despite the squareness of outline, it is just possible to regard the construction of the theme as "ternary" (A, 1-8, B, 9-12, C, 13-8), but whether such a view is

completely justified is open to question. Since the day
when musicians commenced to deride those analysts
who regarded the sonata design as a binary plan, there
has been a marked tendency in some circles to find the
three-part design in everything.   In the perfect ternary
conception there are three points : statement—diversity
—restatement; and it is doubtful if those impressions
are created by the present theme.   The plan here is a
four-bar phrase ending with a half-close followed by
a responsive section closely allied to the fore phrase
but ending with a full close.   Then, instead of a repetition of the original fore phrase, fresh matter is
substituted and the after* phrase repeated with a
codetta-like extension on this plan : A/B : C/B +
approximating in a great degree to the more familiar
binary formula A/B : A/C. All this as a protest
against the use of the description "ternary" on the
slightest provocation !

The theme is a delightful musical moment : if cor-
rectly interpreted. The opening group of quavers
should be regarded as beginning on the half-bar and
swinging rhythmically up to the note E which takes
the main accent. This accentuation leads to a more
correct placing of the cadence chords. It is unneces-
sary to dwell upon the variations of the melody. If
Mozart had been content to write them with a beat

---

* The thematic construction of the "air" attached to Sonata No. 6 and the repetition of the *fore*-phrase lead one to
regard that plan as ternary : the cases are not parallel.

unit that would not have involved the use of those fearsome-looking notes with the four or five tails they might be more often played, and so possibly deeper beauties be revealed.

SECOND MOVEMENT.

The structure of the minuetto is that of the usual ternary design, but the trio is more interesting. The first part is a sentence of sixteen bars modulating to the key of the dominant. The middle portion has the idea of the first section in the key of E minor; and after a few weak bars the second section of the minuetto is recalled, first in C major and then in D minor. While the purpose of the trio is to supply the element of contrast, the introduction in the trio of part of the matter of the minuetto is not without force, for it lends a touch of unity to the movement as a whole. The return to the opening section of the trio is charmingly effected.

THIRD MOVEMENT.

This movement is usually described as a rondo, but would, in fact, be more accurately designated "ternary"; and for this reason: that the sentence of digression opening in the relative major key (bars 9 (*b*)-17) is again employed, whereas the episodes in a rondo form proper differ completely.

The period of digression is somewhat irregular in construction, although the repetition of the A major portion lends cohesion to the section. After the re-

capitulation of the opening section, a part of the episode—that previously referred to—is again recalled
and is followed by a lengthy coda.   My pen had
almost written "*leads* to the coda," but here is no in-
sinuative introduction; for the concluding part is most
unhappily added in a fashion which recalls the hood-
winked efforts in the "tail-less donkey game" of
youthful days!   The matter of this movement taken
in view of its title makes curious reading to-day, when
men in our midst have produced compositions which
so wonderfully reflect the spirit and exhale the heavy
perfumes of the East.

SONATA NO. 12, IN F MAJOR.

SONATA NO. 12, IN F MAJOR.
(Zimmermann Edition.)

First movement, "Allegro." Key, F major. Form, sonata.

Exposition: 1-22, first subject; 22³-40, bridge passage; 41-56, 56-70, 71-86, 86-93, second subject. Development: 94-132. Recapitulation: 133-54, first subject; 154-76, bridge passage; 177-229, second subject.

Second movement, "Adagio." Key, B flat major. Form, modified sonata.

Exposition: 1-8, first subject; 9-19, second subject. Development: 19-20. Recapitulation: 21-8, first subject; 29-39, second subject; 39-40, coda.

Third movement, "Assai Allegro." Key, F major. Form, sonata.

Exposition: 1-35, first subject; 36-49, bridge passage; 50-65, 65-85, 85-90, second subject in dominant minor. Development: 91-147. Recapitulation: 148-69, first subject; 169-84, bridge passage; 185-226, second subject (tonic minor); 227-45, coda.

First Movement.

The music of the exposition is broken into its several parts by the bold opening of the bridge passage in the key of D minor. The development section opens with matter which suggests the second subject; and later the second section of that subject is employed. The transitions are to C minor, G minor, D minor and back to F major.

Second Movement.

The first subject moves from the tonic key to F minor, ending with a tierce de Picardie which serves to introduce the new key. It should be noted that the cadence points indicate wrong barring; and with $\frac{2}{4}$ as a time signature the theme would be of the more orthodox sixteen-bar construction (see note on the first movement of the previous sonata). There is no development. Two bars over a dominant pedal lead back to the tonic key. Both subjects, as is usual in this form, are ornamented on their reappearance.

Third Movement.

This is a movement which brings to mind some of the concluding movements of the pianoforte sonatas of Beethoven. The convincing rhythmic swing, the excellent disposition and construction of the thematic material, the careful timing and planning of episodical periods—all these things are as evident here as in the works of the later master; but still there is a "something" lacking. The weakness lies in the harmonic basis. Examine the first line of this particular movement. What do we find? Simply an ornamentation of the tonic harmony with each note of the chord taken in turn as the pivot upon which a time group centres. When in performance these time groups are converted into rhythmic groups by correct phrasing, there is still no sense of progression. I am reminded of a story. Shall I tell it to you?

In the small hours of the morning a man passing the entrance to a block of flats espied a gentleman [*sic*] attired in evening dress seated disconsolately on the stairs. He felt that he must act the "good samaritan," and so proffered his assistance in negotiating the stairway. All the information he could obtain was "First floor—first door." Arrived at that point, and not wishing to encounter a possible and angry woman who might jump to wrong conclusions as to his share in the business, he thrust the helpless man inside the door and hurried away. Judge of his amazement when he came upon another form in dress attire and evidently sadly in need of assistance lying at almost the same spot. Feeling that this must be his busy day, he extended to this man a similar good service. Profuse in his thanks, the merry gentleman asserted that he desired to reach the first door on the first floor. The samaritan even more hurriedly than before accomplished his self-imposed task, and made for escape. As he reached the entrance, a man picked himself up and rather unsteadily fled; and moved by curiosity our obliging friend took up the chase. He began to understand things when he came up to the man whose conduct seemed suspicious, in the very act of embracing a police officer and pleading "Save me from this man. He's thrown me down the lift shaft twice ! ! !" That is the feeling in this music. There is no effective movement; and the dominant harmony at bar 6 only prepares the way for a repetition of the elaborated tonic chord. Now take down your Beethoven and play the opening bars of the last movement of the pianoforte Sonata, Op. 26, noting the wonderful colouring, the rapid harmonic changes, the definite sense of progression which is created with every alternate note, and you will at once realise where the earlier master failed.

The first subject consists of three sections (1-14, 14-22, 22-35): this is unusual in Mozart.

The second subject opens with a sixteen-bar sentence of regular construction in the minor mode of the dominant. The similarity between this subject and the second section of the first theme which has been noted by some writers, is more apparent than real.

At the opening of the final portion only the first two sections of the first subject are recapitulated. The second subject then appears transposed to the tonic key, the minor mode being preserved. Then occurs a reference to the third section of the first subject (previously omitted). This tardy and irregular recapitulation of the exposition matter is also to be noted in the first movement of Sonata No. 19, in D major (q.v.).

SONATA NO. 13, IN B FLAT.

SONATA NO. 13, IN B FLAT.

(Zimmermann Edition.)

First movement, "Allegro." Key, B flat. Form, sonata.
Exposition: $1\text{-}11^4$, first subject; 11-23, bridge passage; 24-39, 40-51, 51-60, 60-4, second subject. Development: 64-94. Recapitulation: 94-104, first subject; 104-19, bridge passage; 120-66, second subject.

Second movement, "Andante Cantabile." Key, E flat. Form, sonata.
Exposition: $1\text{-}8^1$, first subject; 8-13, bridge passage; $13^2\text{-}29$, second subject; 29-31, codetta. Development: $31^2\text{-}50$. Recapitulation: $51^1\text{-}8^1$, first subject; 58-63, bridge passage; $63^2\text{-}79$, second subject in tonic; 79-82, codetta.

Third movement, "Allegretto Grazioso." Key, B flat. Form, rondo-sonata.
Exposition: $1\text{-}16^2$, principal subject; $16\text{-}24^2$, bridge passage; $24\text{-}36^1$, second subject in dominant; $36^2\text{-}40^4$, link; $41\text{-}56^2$, principal subject; 56-64, transition. Episode, 64-111. Recapitulation: 112-27; principal subject, 127-48; bridge passage, 148-64; second subject in tonic; 164-98, link; 199-213. principal subject; 213-24, coda.

First Movement.

Number thirteen! and a most excellent number; for the three movements are interesting and equal. The edition chosen presents the sonatas chronologically, and one feels the fascination of such ordered consideration of the composer's work. The division into periods is not sharply marked as in the case of his great successor; but with this sonata we reach the midway point in the development of Mozart, so far as the pianoforte sonatas are concerned. The evidence of this is: (1) the nature of the bridge passage, which is a continuation of the thought expressed in, and grows out of the previous matter; (2) the strong contrast of the themes: in many of the sonatas the second subject is not totally unlike the principal theme, but this sonata marks a sure advance from Haydn; (3) the middle section contains definite thematic development; and even the bars 89-94, which form a link on dominant harmony, are suggestive of the subject-matter. Undoubtedly this is one of, if not *the* strongest opening movements we have so far dwelt upon.

Second Movement.

This movement is indeed a jewel; for it is firm in construction, harmonically fresh and marked by that beauty of melodic outline which is justly called *Mozartian*. The music provides many instances of a full development of short motives. In the development section the ornamentation of the thematic material leads to the employment of several curious harmonic combinations.*

The first subject is an eight-bar sentence of obvious construction ending with a full close, but where does the second subject begin? At bar 13 with the arpeggio group in the bass, or with the melody which opens at bar 14? Dealing with an earlier sonata I protested against attempts to ignore short passages lying between themes. Such passages have to be played; and the executant has the right to demand of the analyst some guidance in the matter. In this particular case the close at bar 13 is typically *Mozartian* and we can imagine the following quaver group as a 'cello part swinging on to the low B flat on the first beat of bar 14 where the violins (overlapping) enter with a theme. The few notes are not supplementary to the first subject, nor do they form an integral part of the second theme, while further, I do not believe that there exists anywhere a passage which is purely of an intermediate nature! Truth to tell, there is something wrong, something violating the artistic line in such a passage: it reminds me of a chair that, having broken at the back, has been repaired by a joiner; and the wretched man has placed utility before beauty and screwed a hideous metal strip over the break. Have I written much and helped you but little? Well, I

---

* In Mozart's day, many of his MSS. were returned from Italy as "so full of misprints as to be unplayable."

am sorry; but if one begins to pursue these matters
they end by attempting to teach the great creators of
music how to compose.

THIRD MOVEMENT.

A sonata in which the first movement is marked by
vivacity and artistry, with a middle movement full of
beauty and solace, has a worthy finale in a rondo which,
while exceedingly strong in construction and well-knit,
is yet bright, engaging and musical. Many learned
writers have borne testimony to Mozart's grasp of
scientific resource. Now the weakness of the development sections in these sonatas does not seem to merit
this appreciation; but such a conclusion would be er-
roneous. The hand that penned and planned the
"Jupiter" symphony is evident at the opening of this
movement: but in a different form. Here the opening
subject is practically in but two parts throughout. Play
over this matter and realise the force, the richness, the
concentration. This is counterpoint! I would like to
repeat those three words three times, placing an emphasis on each word in turn.

The principal subject is an eight-bar sentence repeated with slightly varied ending; and taking the
two-bar rhythm as the unit, its construction is shown
by the following formula: A/B/A/C/A/B/C/D: an
ideal rondo subject. The second subject is a twelve-
bar theme opening on dominant seventh harmony (third
inversion) in the new key. So far as memory serves
this is the only instance in these sonatas where a sub-

ject opens on harmony other than the tonic of the key
in which the theme is written: a stepping-stone to the
delightfully fresh openings of some Beethoven movements. After the return of the principal theme there
occurs a transition to the key of the episode. It is interesting to note that while in the rondo-sonata form
as at present established the episode in the new key
boldly and immediately succeeds the close of the principal subject, Mozart almost invariably provides a few
bars of transition to the key of the episode. This passage is based upon the bridge passage (bars 16 *et seq.*).
The episode opens in G minor with an eight-bar phrase
and after a short transitional passage a new theme in
the key of E flat is introduced: this gives place to a
limited development of the principal subject; and an
extension of the link used in the exposition leads to
the recapitulation. In this section the bridge passage
moves out to C minor and back to B flat major. It is
based upon the previous links. Occasion may be taken
at this juncture to note a great point of difference
between the old and modern rondo plans. In the older
form the episodes were each different and afforded the
only means of relief; but in the modern design, of
which this number is a notable example, the connecting
matter is frequently founded entirely upon the passage which separates the appearance of the two themes.
Following the representation of the second subject (extended) in the tonic key, a passage appears (164-98)
which partakes of the nature of an extended cadenza.

Fragments of the principal theme are recalled in both major and minor modes, and after some considerable "working up" the theme is finally given, subject to modification. The coda appears to hover between the tonic and subdominant keys.

SONATA NO. 14, IN C MINOR.

SONATA NO. 14, IN C MINOR.

(Zimmermann Edition.)

First movement, "Molto Allegro." Key, C minor. form, sonata.

Exposition: 1-19^1, first subject; 19-22, bridge passage; 23-35, 36-59, 59-67, 67-71, second subject; 71-4, link. Development: 75-99^1. Recapitulation: 100-18, first subject; 118-20, bridge passage; 121-68, second subject in tonic; 168-85, coda.

Second movement, "Adagio." Key, E flat. Form, old rondo.

Part I: 1-7^3, subject; 8-16, episode in dominant; 16, link; 17-23, subject (varied). Part II: 24-40, second and chief episode in A flat. Part III: 41-7, subject; 47^4-57, coda.

Third movement, "Assai Allegro." Key, C minor. Form, modified rondo-sonata.

Exposition: 1-45, principal subject; 46, bridge passage; 47-97^1, second subject in relative major; 97-103^1, link; 104-42, principal subject: 143-6, transition. Episode: 147-67^1. Recapitulation: 168-220, second subject in tonic; 220-71, principal subject; 273-32, coda.

FANTASIA.

May I venture another story? A Scotchman had acquired a great encyclopædia, and a friend who became aware of the purchase asked him how he liked his new treasury of information. The Scotchman replied: "It's grand, man, only it changes the subject so often!" The fantasia is quite like that. Theme after theme succeed each other at first with freshness which later becomes a bewildering and unsettling profusion. Apart from the presentation of the themes in various keys and the development of the initial figure of the "andantino" section, the only touch of unity and cohesion is that imparted by the résumé of the opening theme as a coda. An examination in detail will reveal to the student much of the beauty of masterly treatment, unaffected imitation and interesting harmonic progressions.

FIRST MOVEMENT.

The first subject ends with the perfect close at bar 19. The construction is clear: two four-bar phrases are responded to by an eight-bar phrase which is extended by a repetition of bars 9-13. Note the double counterpoint at the octave (bars 9^4-13^2). Reading over these bars I seemed to know them: and not in connection with Mozart. Will you take down your volume of Beethoven once again and examine bars 9^3-15 of the last movement of Op. 31, No. 1: the comparison is delightfully interesting.

The bridge passage (overlapping the theme) enters with the opening figure. The second subject has four sections, each in the relative key of E flat major. Bars 71-4 form a link founded upon the principal subject leading first to the repetition of the exposition, and later to the development section. In the middle portion the opening section of the second subject, together with the bridge passage, provides the material. Beginning with the opening motive on the dominant harmony of F minor, the key of G minor is also employed before a return is made to the tonic key. In the recapitulation the bridge passage is altered. Note the use of the chord known as the Neapolitan sixth (bar 120) as a means of modulation : approached as that chord in C minor it is quitted as tonic harmony in D flat. Then occurs an interesting departure from regularity. Fresh material in the key of D flat is introduced, evidently substituted for the opening section of the subject (bars 23 *et seq.*); for merging into the matter with which that section closed, it is succeeded by the other sections of the subject in the tonic minor key. It is, I suppose, but artistic justice that the omitted section is the only portion of the second subject which is employed in the development. The coda is based upon the initial figure of the main subject and is (for Mozart) rather lengthy. Another stepping-stone to the wonderful "summing up" of Beethoven.

SECOND MOVEMENT.

An "adagio" bristling with semidemisemiquavers!
The custom of the older composers to so reduce the beat
unit is inexplicable. Had Mozart written the notes with
half the number of tails and doubled the number of
bar lines he would have saved not only his own ink,
but also the time and patience of thousands upon thousands of music-lovers.

The movement is written in old rondo form; and reference has already been made to the rarity of such
employment. The theme is varied or ornamented on
each reappearance. A coda is founded upon the theme
and first episode.

FINALE.

This movement rivals in humour any of the scherzos
of Beethoven. Of course the music should be written
in $\frac{6}{8}$, commencing on the last quaver. It is obvious that
the placing of an equally strong accent on every bar
would be a drag on the wheel and rob the music of
its joyous spirit. We must in effect erase the second
and alternate bar lines. The principal subject is presented in delightful fashion. Some theorists have declared that there are three sections in this matter; but
it cannot be gainsaid that there is only one thought,
the digressions and interruptions serving but to increase
the capricious element. The place of the bridge passage is filled by a solitary chord of the dominant
seventh. This is a wonderful touch; for the short sharp

utterance exerts as it were a steadying influence and prepares, or rather compels, the mind and ear to assume the receptivity necessary for the more sustained matter of the secondary subject. One is lost between admiration of Mozart the musician and Mozart the psychologist !

The second subject is in the key of the relative major. Presented in two sections, the second is mainly cadential in character. Some passage-work leads to the return of the principal subject which is cut short at bar 142 (the equivalent of bar 39 in the exposition). The harmonic progression here is interesting. The interruption of the theme occurs on the dominant seventh (first inversion) harmony in the tonic key; and this being treated as a chromatic supertonic seventh in the key of F minor, is resolved through a dominant minor ninth in the new key. The middle section is short and unimportant. Opening in the key of F minor, the phrase is repeated in G minor and thence to dominant harmony in the original key of C minor. The recapitulatory section begins with the *second* subject (hence the qualification "modified") transposed to the tonic key of C minor; and indeed the whole of the section is delightfully irregular. Instead of an exact repetition of the second section of the second subject the music merges into a link which suggests the principal theme taken by inversion. The inversion is neither exact nor sustained : still the point is there. When the first subject is finally presented it receives almost cadenza-like treatment. Again the course of the theme is interrupted at the spread chords to be succeeded by the matter of the middle portion. Here Mozart picks up the thread of the end of the secondary subject which was broken at bar 212. The sustained notes toward the end of the movement suggest the conclusion of the principal theme.

SONATA NO. 15, IN F MAJOR.

SONATA NO. 15, IN F MAJOR.

(Zimmermann Edition.)

First movement, "Allegro." Key, F. Form, sonata.
Exposition: 1^2-9, first subject; 9^2-42^1. Bridge passage; 42-58, 58-67, 67-90, 90-103, second subject. Development: 103-46. Recapitulation: 146^2-54, first subject; 154^2-69, bridge passage; 169-240, second subject in tonic.

Second movement, "Andante." Key, B flat. Form, sonata.

Exposition: 1-10, first subject; 11-22, bridge passage; 23-33, 33-46, second subject. Development: 47-72^1. Recapitulation: 73-82, first subject; 83-90, bridge passage; 91-114, second subject; 114-22, coda.

Third movement, "Allegretto." Key, F major. Form, modified rondo-sonata.

Exposition: 1-12, principal subject; 13-8, bridge passage; 18-34, second subject; 34-8, link; 39-50, principal subject; 51-79, 79-82, link; 83-94, principal subject. Episode: 95-119. Recapitulation: 120-31, principal subject; 132-43, second subject in tonic; 143-51, link; 152-75, transition; 176-84, principal subject; 184-7, coda.

FIRST MOVEMENT.

The marked rhythm, definite tonality and regular
construction of the main subject when added to the
melodic entry suggest a fugal treatment; and therefore
the examples of double counterpoint and canonic imitation which occur later are especially interesting.
Mozart, unlike Beethoven, does not employ the fugal
form in any of the pianoforte sonatas. The bridge
passage is a development of the subject matter. As the
tonic key is not quitted until bar 33, some theorists
might consider that the principal subject extends to
the first beat in that bar (33); and that it is curtailed
in the recapitulation. It is perhaps clearer to regard
the subject as ending at bar 9, while the bridge passage
is subject to curtailment in the final section; and this
is the reasoning (or is it only a feeling) that leads to
such a conclusion. It is quite easy to imagine Mozart
revelling in this subject in the early part of the movement, but after such a lengthy treatment in the exposition and considerable development in the free fantasia
section, the composer wisely reduces the matter in the
recapitulation. The development section employs the
first subject and also the first section of the second
subject. Opening in C minor the music passes througb
G minor, D minor, back to G minor, to C major, and
so to the original tonality. Note the employment of
the second subject at the twelfth (bar 134) and at the
octave (bar 136). As previously stated, the bridge pas-

sage is considerably curtailed and contains rapid modulations to keys so far removed as D flat major and B flat minor. The establishment of the key of D flat at this point is interesting when regarded in conjunction with the harmonic progression at bar 41. The use of the second portion of the second subject as a counter-theme to the principal subject is good (bars 202 *et seq.*).

Second Movement.

This is a wonderful little movement although the harmonies are at times somewhat strained. The first subject ends on dominant harmony at bar 10. The fore phrase of four bars ends with an inverted perfect cadence; and the after phrase is extended (bars 6^3-8^2) by sequential treatment. The bridge passage continues the thought of the opening theme. In the development section the initial notes of the second subject are thrown about from one hand to the other accompanied by chromatic runs. Some beautiful harmonic progressions suggestive of the first subject lead to the recapitulation. The coda is based upon a figure derived from the second subject (bar 107).

Finale.

The principal theme, consisting of two equally balanced phrases, extends to twelve bars. The link grows out of the subject. The second subject in the key of the dominant opens on subdominant harmony. Here again a link seems to re-echo the thought of the subject which it follows; and the principal subject (to which it leads) is varied. Ordinarily the exposition should end here; for we have had themes declared to be first subject, connecting passage, secondary theme in related key, a retransition to, and restatement of, the principal subject. While I am not disposed to argue with those who hold that the exposition *does* conclude at bar 50, I cannot agree with them; and even at the risk of appearing inconsistent in departing from definitions to which I have previously subscribed, I must be honest to myself. There is a view which I like better; and it is expressed in the above analysis. After bar 50 there is an episode (50-82) opening boldly in D minor, which, passing through B flat major and G minor, leads to the *third* appearance of the principal subject, concluding the first portion of the movement. Then follows the central episode. At first glance this may appear to be so short as to be out of proportion to the other parts of the movement; but in such a matter—whatever we may be content to do in performance—we cannot overlook the repeat marks. If I protest much further my readers will think that I should have been a labour orator rather than a writer on matters musical, but the mention of repeat marks leads me to state that in many cases executants in their desire to reduce the time of performance freely and lightly ignore such marks; and thereby venture to materially depart from the plan as conceived and laid down by the composer. Take the episode which we are at the moment considering. Without repeats it is a simple ternary structure (A-B-A [2]); and as we have already noted, becomes too

brief : but with the repetitions it partakes of the nature
of a free simple rondo design; and is fairly propor-
tioned to the general scheme.   I take it that you have
noted that the main theme of this episode recurs in the
bass at bar 109!   After the recapitulation of the principal subject the second theme enters duly transposed
to the tonic key; but its course is interrupted to make
way for a transition in fugato style which, while irregular, is distinctly welcome.   The theme with a contrapuntal bass concludes the movement, the coda being
simply cadential.

SONATA NO. 16, IN C MAJOR.

SONATA NO. 16, IN C MAJOR.

(Zimmermann Edition.)

First movement, "Allegro." Key C. Form, sonata.
Exposition: bars 1-12, first subject; 13-26, 26-8, second subject. Development: 29-41. Recapitulation: 42-57, first subject; 58-73, second subject.

Second movement, "Andante." Key, G major. Form, ternary.

Part I: bars 1-32; Part II: 33-48; Part III: 49-64, 64-74.

Third movement, "Allegretto." Key, C major. Form, old rondo.

Bars 1-9, principal subject; 9-17, episode in dominant; 17-21, link; 21-9, subject; 29-52, chief and longest episode in A minor; 53-61, subject; 61-74, coda.

First Movement.

This number is of course a sonatina written for the young. It presents, however, several points of interest. The first subject ends with a *half close* at bar 12. The simplicity and effectiveness of the means by which the new key sense is created is deserving of passing notice.

The middle section is based upon the concluding section (26-8) of the second subject and is episodical. This sounds somewhat paradoxical; but of course these two bars consist merely of the broken chords of the tonic and dominant. This progression is reproduced in the keys of G, D and A, the minor mode being employed in each case. At bar 40^3 the transition is effected to F major. The recapitulation also provides an interesting departure from regularity: Mozart presents the first subject in the subdominant key. Prout says: that the object of this unusual procedure is that the key relationships of the first and second subjects may be the same as in the exposition; but the expediency appears to be at least doubtful, as the effect of beginning the recapitulation in a key other than the tonic is hardly satisfactory. In the ternary form of which the sonata form is a variation, the return of the tonic key is one of the chief characteristics of the third part. There is a slight extension owing to the necessity of establishing the tonic key. Note the melodic change (with rhythmic preservation) at bars 67-8.

SECOND MOVEMENT.

This is a curious structure: in some lights it seems like a rondo; but perhaps *ternary* is the most fitting description. The thematic outline is in itself somewhat monotonous. The first part consists of two sixteen-bar sections. There occurs a half close at bar 8 when the matter is repeated with some elaboration until a perfect cadence is reached at bar 16. The second section opens in the key of D major with matter much akin to that already heard, and after a close in that key a short re-transition leads to a repetition of the initial phrase in the original key. The episode is neither more nor less than a free translation of the thematic material of the first part in the minor mode of several keys; and is succeeded by a retrospection of the first section of Part I, followed by a coda. The faults are: the weakness of the thematic foundation and the lack of the element of contrast. The only evidence of design lies in the key-scheme.

FINALE.

This movement is practically identical in form and matter with the last movement of Sonata No. 17, in F major. It is described as a rondo, but might be regarded as an example of ternary form: Part I, bars 1-29; Part II, 29-52; Part III, 53-74. The lack of contrast in the episodes lends support to this view. It would be interesting to know how this movement comes to be duplicated. It is hardly possible to believe that Mozart with his marvellous powers of invention would have so repeated himself; and yet history tells us of the strange happenings to many compositions of the great masters. It makes one feel like the Bible student who desires to see the original epistles in the handwriting of St. Paul. May I grow reminiscent for just a moment? What I am going to say has nothing, or at best, very little concern with musical design, but whenever I see this movement my mind goes back to the day when, as a young student, I tried my prentice hand at composition. This movement was my model; and when my rondo was complete and carefully re-copied I ventured to show it to a head professor at a college where they endeavoured to instruct me in the principles of my art. Now this professor enjoyed a great and mighty reputation, but he had, I am sure, passed the allotted three score and ten; and, moreover, although still exerting himself over his professorial duties, was growing as blind as a bat. I awaited his verdict with considerable interest and trepidation. I was found "not guilty"; and indeed kind words of encouragement and benediction fell from the lips of the judge. So flattering were his remarks that I had not the heart to inform him that he had been looking at my Opus I *upside down*!

SONATA NO. 17, IN F MAJOR.

SONATA NO 17, IN F MAJOR.
(Zimmermann Edition.)

First movement, "Allegro." Key, F major. Form, sonata.

Exposition : bars 1-16, first subject; 16-31, bridge passage; 32-64, 64-78, second subject. Development : 79-118. Recapitulation: 119-34, first subject; 134-49, bridge passage; 150-96, second subject.

Second movement, "Allegretto." Key, F major. Form, old rondo.

Part I : bars 1-9, subject; 9-17, episode in dominant key; 17-21, link; 21-9, subject. Part II : 29-52, chief and longest episode in relative minor. Part III : 53-61, subject; 61-76, coda.

The Zimmermann edition declares that the date of composition of this sonata is unknown. The first movement is curiously unequal. The opening theme leads to nowhere. It is again the story of the good Samaritan and the lift shaft; for bars 1-4 and 9-12 are tonic harmony elaborated by auxiliary notes and bye-tones. It is possible to regard the whole of the

matter up to bar 31 as first subject. The remainder
of the exposition is both disconnected and restless. It
is somewhat difficult to exactly define the limits of
the various sections. At first glance there appears to
be four or five contrasted sections, e.g., 32-45, 46-54,
54-64, 64-76, 76-8; but a closer examination shows that
bars 46-54 may readily be considered as a corollary,
and bars 54-64 a passage in the nature of a codetta
or supplementary phrase—the whole constituting a
complete section. Bars 64-76 form the second section,
with the two following bars again as codetta. The
development of the second section of the second subject in the middle section is interesting.

SECOND MOVEMENT.

Compare this movement with the rondo attached to
Sonata No. 16, and see notes thereon (page 125).

SONATA NO. 18, IN B FLAT MAJOR.

SONATA NO. 18, IN B FLAT MAJOR.

(*Zimmermann Edition.*)

First movement, "Allegro." Key, B flat. Form, sonata.

Exposition: bars 1-20, first subject; 21-40, bridge passage; 41-57, 57-69, 70-9, second subject. Development: 80-132. Recapitulation: 133-52, first subject; 153-70, bridge passage; 171-209, second subject.

Second movement, "Adagio." Key, E flat. Form, ternary.

Part I: bars 1-12. Part II, 13-28. Part III: 29-56.

Third movement, "Allegretto." Key, B flat. Form, rondo.

Part I: bars 1-9, subject; 9-15, link; 16-23, subject. Part II: 23-63. Part III: 64-71, subject; 71-90, coda.

FIRST MOVEMENT.

The first subject is interesting; for the thought is more definite and more completely expressed than in many of the preceding sonatas. The bars 21-2 which open the bridge passage are strikingly succeeded by a new and distinct theme in the key of E flat. The quickening of the movement at bar 35 is rather inexplicable. The second theme combines, with the happiest effect, the two figures used in the construction of the first subject. The development section opens with a sudden transition to the key of D flat, in which key the matter of the bridge passage is introduced, The second subject is also employed with an invertible counterpoint. The return of the first subject is most insinuating and the reappearance of the transposed second subject clearly reveals the opening of the two themes as identical.

SECOND MOVEMENT.

This rondo-like movement bears a similarity in structure to the Rondo alla Turca with which the Sonata No. 11 closes (q.v.). The first portion consists of the theme (bars 1-4) followed by a theme of digression and a repetition of the first bars, making with repeats a miniature rondo form without dissimilarity in the episodes. The episode is similar in construction, but contrasted in tonality and style. Opening in C minor, a section of four bars is succeeded by one of equal length which leads from F minor to C minor and a repetition of the C minor theme. Bars 25-8 form a link to the final part which opens with a repetition of the main motive, but, in place of the short sentence of digression, there is a new episode consisting of two sections followed (bars 41-4) by a link leading to the final appearance of the theme at bar 45.

THIRD MOVEMENT.

The principal subject ends at bar 9; and is founded entirely upon the harmonies of the tonic and dominant, save for the use of Mozart's usual cadence—II, V, I. It is succeeded by a passage in the dominant key which must be regarded as a link. The use of this key at this point is, however, noteworthy; for it foreshadows the introduction of the second subject in the new rondo form. The episode consists of several sections. The first section (23-31) opens in B flat and modulates to the dominant key : the second begins directly in C minor and returns to B flat. Bars 43-5 form a link, derived from bar 9^4, to the key of E flat. The passage 46-57 is quite contrasted in character, and bars 14-6 are referred to before the final appearance of the subject. The coda is lengthy and employs the syncopated figure of the episode.

SONATA NO. 19, IN D MAJOR.

SONATA NO. 19, IN D MAJOR.

(*Zimmermann Edition.*)

First movement, "Allegro." Key, D. Form, sonata.

Exposition: 1-17, first subject; 17-42, bridge passage; 42-54, 54-9, second subject. Development: 60-99. Recapitulation: 99-107, first subject; 107-22, bridge passage; 122-61, second subject.

Second movement, "Adagio." Key, A. Form, ternary.

Part I: bars 1-16. Part II: 17-43. Part III: 44-59. Coda: 59-67.

Third movement, "Allegretto." Key, D. Form, modified rondo-sonata.

Exposition: bars 1-16, principal subject; 16-25, bridge passage; 26-50, 50-8, second subject; 58-64, link; 65-80, principal subject; episode, 80-116. Recapitulation: 117-49, second subject; 149-62, link; 163-78, principal subject; coda, 178-89.

FIRST MOVEMENT.

As in the sonatas Nos. 6 and 20 (q.v.), the subject might end at bar 9 or 17: it is a matter of some uncertainty and for personal choice. In this case there is a full close in the tonic key at both points. The recapitulatory section only reproduces the first nine bars; but as that section contains other irregularities too much importance must not be attached thereto. The bridge passage also presents a problem. Analysed as above it contains two sections, 17-28 and 28-42. Now at bar 28 the new key is not definitely reached. True, the composer has made a spring-board from which it is possible to dive into the new key; but it seems as if Mozart, feeling the lack of key stability, has proceeded to confirm the dominant tonality. That he should definitely and muchly use that key was inevitable. Another point which may account for the length of this section is the nature of the subject, and the imitational device. The alternative plan is to regard the second subject as commencing at bar 28; but personally, the affinity of this matter to the first subject theme, together with the omission or displacement in the recapitulatory section prevents me adopting this view. The development section provides some examples of canonic imitation. Prout says: "Next to Sebastian Bach no one has shown greater mastery of scientific resources." Opening in A minor, the music quickly passes to B flat major, thence to G minor, B minor and D major. It is curious to note the several references to the two concluding bars of the exposition; although apparently the same as the opening phrase they *feel* quite different. Only the first portion of the bridge passage is at first recapitulated; but at bar

139 a further irregularity is to be noted: the second portion of the bridge (previously omitted) is interpolated between the second subject matter.

SECOND MOVEMENT.

Here is a delightful example of the Mozart slow movement, and one would wish that it had been, or still might be written in $\frac{3}{2}$ time. In the present form the notational difficulties far exceed the technical demands; and consequently the student is debarred from intimacy until perchance his tastes and inclinations tend toward music of a more bizarre character. A more rational edition of Mozart might lead some, who now lightly and inadvisedly ignore these works, to more fully appreciate their wholesome tone, simple beauty and absolute purity.

THIRD MOVEMENT.

In the first movement of Sonata No. 18 we noted that the opening of the second subject was similar to that of the first theme; but with a fresh counter-subject. Here is a parallel case. This renewed lack of contrast between the themes is perplexing: either we admit retrogression on the part of the master, or doubt the authenticity of the dates of composition usually assigned to the later numbers; and I prefer to be a Thomas. Sonata No. 17 is weak and doubtless due to the artfulness of some "early and unknown editor": the finale of No. 18 is patently less mature than that attached to, e.g., either Sonata 13 or 15: indeed we never seem to pick up that thread of development which was broken by the Sonatina No. 16. The episode opens with the use of the bridge passage, and contains many references to the second subject (*which is identified as such by the counter-subject*) in various keys. As in the last movement of the Sonata No. 7, in C major (q.v.) the recapitulation opens with the *second* subject. Bars 149-62 form a rather extended link. It is possible to regard bars 149-89 as coda (as I believe Prout has done); but as bars 163-78 present the principal subject in its original form, the analysis here outlined would seem to more closely adhere to the regular construction.

SONATA NO. 20, IN B FLAT MAJOR.

SONATA NO. 20, IN B FLAT MAJOR.

(Zimmermann Edition.)

First movement, "Allegro." Key, B flat. Form, sonata.

Exposition: bars 1-9, first subject; 9-33, bridge passage; 33-43, 43-54, 54-8, second subject. Development: 59-85. Recapitulation: 85-93, first subject; 93-108, bridge passage; 108-33, second subject.

Second movement, "Andante." Key, E flat. Form, air with variations.

Third movement, Minuetto and Trio. Keys, B flat and E flat. Form, ternary.

Minuetto: bars 1-9, theme; 9-26, digression; 26-36, theme.

Trio: bars 1-9, theme; 9-17, digression; 17-25, theme. Minuetto da capo.

Fourth movement, "Allegro." Key, B flat. Form, modified rondo-sonata.

Exposition: bars 1-44, principal subject; 44-56, bridge passage; 56-79, second subject in dominant; 79-88, link; 89-104, principal subject. Episode: 104-83. Recapitulation: 184-234, principal subject in tonic key.

This sonata is the only example in the pianoforte sonatas of Mozart where more than three movements are employed. It is not an original work but an arrangement by an "early and unknown editor." If you ask me if he is the editor to whom I referred while examining No. 19, I have to reply that I cannot tell; but, if so, his description reveals a just fate. The analysis has been included here for the sake of completeness; and also for the problem presented by the irregularity and general interest—particularly of the final movement.

First Movement.

The sonata opens with a theme of binary structure, with an imperfect cadence at bar 5. The initial bars are then repeated with the parts inverted while the latter part is amended so as to end with a perfect close. This is succeeded by a sequential passage which, after building up to a strong point, leads to the introduction of the opening theme. The movement bears every evidence of mature thought and sound judgment. The passage at bar 9 may now appear conventional; but it contains the germ of an idea which Beethoven was to develop to a wonderful extent. I refer to those delicious "attempts" at a theme*; and the sequential mounting up to the climax points. Another device that is not too frequently used in these sonatas is the

---

* The same idea is delightfully employed at bars 106-8 previous to the return of the second subject.

evolution of the theme which is exemplified at bars
18 *et seq.* The second subject strongly resembles the
principal theme and in this latter portion of the exposition we seem to glimpse his great successor yet
again. In view of the repeated use of the initial
phrase, the use of the dominant chords at bar 59 is
noteworthy. The composer realising that familiarity
may breed contempt is loathe to open with the matter
at bar 60; but the reiterated staccato chords rivet the
attention and gain for the development section its
due measure of attention. As one closes the movement the early Beethoven is very clearly sensed.

Second Movement.

This movement is declared to be arranged from a
concerto (1784). While the minor mode is not directly
employed, it is very skilfully suggested in the latter
portion of the final variation.

Third Movement.

Both minuetto and trio are built upon ternary plans;
and in both alike the sentence of digression bears that
"family likeness" to the main theme. The development contained in the middle part of the minuetto
deserves more than passing attention.

Fourth Movement.

The construction of this movement is not by any
means regular. It doubtless belongs to the transition
period, but it is possible to trace the main divisions.

The principal subject is of considerable length, and in itself is a ternary structure. Bars 1-16 provide the main theme: bars 17-28 the sentence of digression, with (29-40) a repetition of the first phrase followed by (40-4) of a codetta or supplementary nature. The bridge passage opens with a point of imitation in G minor and modulates to F major. The composer has caught up the little codetta to the subject. The second subject is followed by a re-transition to the original key when there is a partial presentation of the principal subject—sufficient, however, to convey the idea of recapitulation. The middle section is of curious construction. Bars 104-9 form a modulation to E flat: bars 109-34 provide an episode of new matter commencing in E flat and modulating to the key of B major (bar 135), where there is much development of the principal theme in that key, and also the key of G. Finally, the music returns to the original tonal centre. The method of these extraneous transitions is worthy of detailed and minute examination. Begin at bar 129 and follow the harmonic course to bar 136, where the key of B major is reached. In this remote key the subject is then announced and passing to G major the theme again appears (bar 162). At bar 176 a re-transition to B flat is cleverly effected. There is a complete review of the main subject which merges (bar 223) into a short but effective coda.

AFTERTHOUGHTS.

That brilliant writer and original thinker, G. K. Chesterton, says in one of his books that "the teacher who does not dogmatise is simply a teacher who does not teach." Now I am deeply conscious of the indefiniteness which has marked my work as analyser of these sonatas; but I rather glory in it. I hate those books on analysis which look like nothing so much as a railway guide; and which are neither provocative of thought nor truly informative. We must remember that it is presumptuous for any other than the creator of an art-work to dogmatise on the plan in detail.

I would exhort every student of musical design to play and replay each work which he is wishful to analyse: or, to listen carefully while someone .else does so. By this means the structure will be revealed. At first, it may be, that only the recapitulatory principle is appreciated: then will come the ability to note the end of the exposition; and that will mean that the three main divisions are recognised. Afterwards, by noting the cadence points and the course of modula

149

tion, we are led to a realisation of the division and extent of the subject matter; and finally—this is dependent upon the power of retention in regard to the thematic material—an insight is gained into the means and devices employed by the composer in securing his more delicate, subtle and minute points of detail. Therefore, play, play, play; *and listen.* Of course it is quite easy for the musician to both play and listen mentally; but this power of mental conception unfortunately is not a general acquirement. It is an incontrovertible fact that the discouragement of the use of the instrument in the early stages has led to the deplorable divorce of theory and practice. The subject of Form, like all other "paper-work," has too often been a blind alley occupation. The wall which makes a cul-de-sac of that which should rightly be a path leading straight on to the broad highway of musical appreciation must be demolished; and the cultivated eye and ear which can create a perfect mental conception are the instruments of destruction. The capable executant is able to build up a work extemporaneously in any mould; and surely the student of design should be able to observe and appreciate the foundation and plan of any art form with equal rapidity and intelligence. Here Mozart may be a most useful study. I conclude with a quotation from a recently published book* : 'Though perhaps not one of the grandest and,

---

* "An Illustrated History of Music." Tapper and Goetschius. (John Murray, 1915.)

intellectually, most powerful of the great masters, Mozart is surely the most amiable character in all music history, as his music is at once the purest and most scholarly. This attribute of musical purity and refinement, proof against the most searching theoretic and æsthetic scrutiny, is the salient trait of his work. . . . . He was as serious, tenacious and thorough in his art as was ever the sternest pedant, but without the slightest taint anywhere of dogmatism or mere scholasticism; his counterpoint is natural because, even when most complex, it seems to unfold as free from technical effort as an improvisation. . . . . Had not Beethoven so soon followed Mozart and overshadowed him with his power of reflecting the tremendous passion of universal human emotion, Mozart's instrumental works would doubtless not have fallen into partial neglect. This is deplorable, but it is a natural consequence of the rapid growth of the art in the early years of the nineteenth century. Nevertheless, there are among Mozart's instrumental creations many that still glow with immortal lustre sufficient to perpetuate his name in the history of the tone art."

LIVERPOOL, *1916.*

INDEX.